# ROBINSON ALONE

Kathleen Rooney

Published by Gold Wake Press

Cover photo by Eric Plattner

ISBN 10: 0-9837001-4-1

ISBN 13: 978-0-9837001-4-2

*Robinson Alone*
Kathleen Rooney
2012

**GOLD Wake Press**

# ROBINSON ALONE

# ACKNOWLEDGEMENTS

Grateful acknowledgement is made to the editors of the publications in which many of these poems originally appeared, sometimes in slightly different form, including:

*Another Chicago Magazine, Antioch Review, Augury Press Blog, The Battersea Review, Cimarron Review, Comstock Review, Diner, Drunken Boat, elimae, Florida Review, Gargoyle, Gettysburg Review, Gigantic Sequins, GW Review, Hotel Amerika, Ilya's Honey, JMWW, Linebreak, Little White Poetry Journal, Locuspoint, Main Street Rag, Night Train, No Tell Motel, Notre Dame Review, Otoliths, PoetsArtists, Sawbuck, SIR!, Subtropics, The Nervous Breakdown, Valparaiso Poetry Review, Word For/*Word*, and Word Riot.*

"Robinson walks Museum Mile" also appeared in *Aspects of Robinson: Homage to Weldon Kees*, an anthology edited by Christopher Buckley and Christopher Howell, and "If Robinson came from the Heartland" also appeared in *A Face to Meet the Faces: An Anthology of Contemporary Persona Poetry*, edited by Stacey Lynn Brown and Oliver de la Paz. "Robinson's Hometown" was also featured on the *InDigest* "Poem of the Day" podcast.

Thanks are due, too, to Kate Clanchy, Elisa Gabbert, Dana Gioia, Elizabeth Hildreth, Jeremy Hoffeld, Brendan Hogan, Caryn Lazzuri, Eric Plattner, Erwin Ponce, Mitchell Rathberger, Martin Seay and Samuel Wharton, and to Carl Annarummo of Greying Ghost Press who published some of these poems in the chapbook *After Robinson Has Gone*. Much gratitude, as well, goes to J. Michael Wahlgren of Gold Wake Press.

NOTE

The biographical information in this collection is drawn from *The Collected Poems of Weldon Kees* edited by Donald Justice, *Vanished Act: The Life and Art of Weldon Kees* by James Reidel, and *Weldon Kees and the Midcentury Generation: Letters, 1935-1955* edited by Robert E. Knoll. The author is grateful to Justice, Reidel, and Knoll, and to the University of Nebraska Press for publishing all three books.

FOR ROSE ROONEY SUPER

# TABLE OF CONTENTS

## II.

## III.

## ROBINSON'S HOMETOWN

has nothing to do with Dante. You say
it with an accent: you say it Be-*at*-trice.

A dirt road lined with leafless trees.
Smokestacks. Some background.

A slight white kid in white kid shoes
& a dress with ruffles & three pearl

buttons. Structures skidded against
the flat flat plains, all rising vertical

sightlines man-grown or man-made.
The corn bursting. The First Presbyterian

Church. The Institution for Feeble-
Minded Youth. The football games

& the Buffalo Bill Street Parade
& Robinson acting in elementary

school plays: Sir Lancelot once,
& Pinocchio, obviously. A little man.

Robinson reading on the family porch.
Torch songs wafting from the nighttime

radio—AM broadcasts lofting
like ghosts from real cities. This

& his mother's artful research—her side
is descended from the Plantagenets,

maybe signed the Magna Carta—&
his suffragette Aunt Clara giving him

a French dictionary for high school
graduation chart it out for Robinson:

most of the world is not in Nebraska.
Robinson lacks patience for too much

prelude, rude though it is to be so
fidgety, ungrateful. This hateful small.

This hateful empty. Civic & dutiful.
Not not beautiful. These moldered.

These elderly. Soon-to-be outgrown.
He simply must. Or bust. A loner

ill-suited to being alone. In a double-
breasted suit. En route to elsewhere.

I.

# ROBINSON SENDS A LETTER TO SOMEONE

*Cento I*

Much to say: don't know how to begin.
Sunday. Berlioz (uneven) on the radio,
with Mr. Enesco or whatever conducting.

The highschool boy across the hall whistles
with quasi-cheer (close the transom,
we can't hear the goddamn Berlioz);

the psychopathic dog downstairs whimpers,
barks, is mildly scolded;
                                        the gas splutters;
dark sky; snow coming they say. A note
to myself is stuck in the mirror: "Remember
to get book at lib." Too many cigarettes.
The old despair. The soot peacefully
floating in the cold afternoon. I'm not
doing what I want to do;
is anyone?                        How to begin?

# IF ROBINSON CAME FROM THE HEARTLAND

then this must be the brainland.
*Do not disappoint*, he demands

of the city. *Do not be fooled*,
he commands himself.

Does he want a master, or
does he want a companion?

Unmusses the bed. Hungover,
he feels the promise of the place;

as well, that the place may break
him like a promise. Pulls back

the lace curtain: the sun burning.
The blank faces. All right—

he's here. But to be near is not
the same as to be close.  Ann,

his wife, must arrive behind him.
*I'm in trouble. Where are you?* he

jokes into the phone. *Another time
zone*, she answers. *How do I*

*know if I'm any good?* he asks,
but the connection's gone bad

& there's only a comfort tone.
He's got to make a plan—

to make a drawing of a hand
without looking at a hand.

## OUT OF STEP WITH HIS GENERATION

what can Robinson generate?

It's too soon to feel surly about finding a salary, but the Chelsea costs three dollars a day.

Combs the classifieds, drinks his coffee.

He's been reclassified: Selective Service 3-A.

Must he fake standing moist-eyed beneath the flag?

Didn't even bring his typewriter to the city.

Likely to be cast in the theater of war.

Hopes he's mistaken.

Steps outside & 360s midtown looking for a sign—

HELP WANTED he has in mind.

WISDOM he finds. As in:

WISDOM AND KNOWLEDGE SHALL BE THE STABILITY OF THY TIMES

on the Radio Corporation of America Building owned by General Electric.

Makes some mental edits:

FOOLISHNESS AND HYSTERIA SHALL BE THE PRECARIOUSNESS OF THY TIMES.

Robinson's feelings about his country are eclectic.

# ROBINSON'S REFRIGERATOR

No butter. No bacon.
No sugar. No meat.
Robinson stands, hand
resting on the open door.
There's a war on.
Inside the icebox,
quiet & deep, lies
a frosty metropolis.
Robinson finds solace
in its small whirring
motor, plays god
with its bare interior
bulb—that always
full moon, that tiny sun.
Robinson can't sleep.
Fanning himself with
chill air, Robinson
waits for a break-
through. The fridge
light coming on—
epiphany—the fridge
light clicking off.

## ROBINSON'S FRIENDS TAKE HIM TO A WESTERN-THEMED BAR

though he's come from afar not to be near the West.

The marquee horse jumps the neon fence

& saddle-shaped barstools line the natural-stone bar.

Robinson addles his head with whiskey.

Jack Delaney's Steak House is lousy with horses—horses, horses, everywhere horses.

Everyone looks risky when the lights are so red.

The sign on the men's room door says: *Colts—Geldings—Studs*.

Which one is Robinson?

A wild night out, a wild night to be wild.

Robinson's friends are high mild questioners

& he listens to their non sequiturs, their sine qua whatevers:

*Why do you always want to fuck when you're drinking?*

*& In vino veritas*

*& That's a big knife & those girls are really drunk.*

He could be home with his Smith Corona.

Instead, he's drinking a Smith & Wesson.

The nags on the walls seem to nag in his ears:

*It'll be a bad night unless you call it a day.*

*Remember, when you fall, you never fall halfway.*

Something's being learned here, but not a lesson.

# ROBINSON SENDS A LETTER TO SOMEONE

*Cento II*

Sorry to be a bit slow in responding
to yr. good communication.
The period during which one waits
for the Army to gobble one up
seems to divide itself neatly
between the terrifying & the full.

It's a changed world: the Albert Hotel
has been taken over by the Army;
the Brevoort is crammed with refugees.
Getty is somewhere in the South Pacific.
Last week I had my blood test & am
wondering what will happen next?

We went to a party. Light
refreshments (liquid) were served.
Everyone said that if you told the draft
board you were a bedwetter
you were a cinch for Class 3D.
We got up with slight hangovers.

I have been looking around
for some sort of job to tide me over
until the Army communicates,
& have discovered what I should have known:
3A men are about as popular as lepers.
One is looked at as already in khaki.

Yet there is a possibility that I may
get a job on *Time*—less exacting
on the draft status matter than most.
I'll probably know definitely this week?
No sacrifice is too great? What do you
think the post-war world will be like?

# ROBINSON FOLLOWS ROBERT'S RULES OF ORDER

The demanding man in the gray flannel suit leans across the table.

Commands: *Laugh,*

& they laugh.

Every time everyone's all in favor, including him, Robinson wants to reply not *Aye*

but: *Nay!*

Why? He doesn't know.

Tragedy ennobles. Comedy cuts down to size.

All in favor? *Aye Aye Aye!*

Parliamentary procedure! Toward what do you proceed?

Did anything worthwhile ever get done at a meeting?

This august institution…

These humans on the board…

Robinson jots inutile notes on a utilitarian pad:

*History is history. It is not moving toward a particular goal*

&

*One has to have irony when dealing with ghosts*

&

*Poor people have bad haircuts & teeth & fat asses & bus passes, but we must love them anyway*

Aye or nay? Aye or nay?

Has Robinson clawed his way to the top? Clawed his way to the middle?

Little shudder. This has to stop.

Does he hear a motion? a motion? a second? Another?

Let's break into small groups & save each other.

## THE WATERFRONT NEAR VINEGAR HILL & FULTON FERRY LANDING

contains Robinson, standing
between the Brooklyn Bridge
& the Manhattan Bridge
Overpass—steel & stone
parentheses framing the city
in what his co-worker/friend/
co-cocktail-party-attender
calls the most majestic man-
made view in human history.
This friend is a blowhard,
though it's hard not to agree.
August light laps the sky-
scrapers like the tongue of a cat.
Mongers hawk their catches
& gulls flipping from the east
& west spans look like someone
spilled a boxful of fake mustaches.
Robinson would like to point out
that a jump from either structure
would scramble your organs
like eggs in a diner. But no one
likes a whiner. He took the F
train to get here. F, he wonders,
for fuck it? Or F for it's fine?
He thinks of his job at *Time*:
cinema editor. How quickly
they hired him. How these
are tough times. How he
should quit before they fire him
because he might get drafted.
But what would that solve?
A train goes by, a wino groans.
Robinson will not take the F
train back. Shadows darken
as the sun climbs.

# ROBINSON WALKS MUSEUM MILE

the ideal city building itself in his brain.
Is this mile magnificent? He's lived here

a while, but the mile feels unreal. Robinson's
training himself to act blasé. Do museums

amuse him? Yes, but not today. Would he
like to be in one? Of course. Why not?

An object of value with canvas wings,
an unchanging face in a gilt frame, arranged—

thoughtless, guilt-free, & preserved
for eternity. Robinson doesn't want to *be*

exceptional. He knows he is. He wants to be
*perceived* exceptional. Trains plunge by, steam

rising from the grates. Sing, muse! of a man
ill-met at the Met. A man on his lunch break,

heading for a heartbreak, a break-up with *Time*.
A break-up with time? Feeling filled with ice,

the way you chill a glass, Robinson passes
the National Academy. He craves a sense

of belonging, not to always be longing. To be
standing in a doorway, incredibly kissable,

not waiting at the four-way, eminently missable.
Is this mile magnanimous? He wants it

unanimous: that this is his kind of town—
up & down & including Brooklyn. The sky

is clearing, but the isolation sticks.
Robinson's not sure what a camera obscura

is for, but he thinks he should have
his portrait done with one. Faces

blur by as he heads toward the Frick.
Something used to photograph the obscure.

# ROBINSON REGARDS THE SNOW BABIES IN CENTRAL PARK

Here the street-noise fades,
grows dark, & Robinson's
hearing becomes more keen
as the sounds of the city turn
vespertine: the soft susurrations
of his seersucker trousers,
the nasal hum of crepuscular bugs.

The stone Snow Babies atop
the beige brick gates—hats on
their heads, sleds at their feet—
look out of place in the mid-
summer heat. He can barely care
for himself. The same goes for
his wife. How could they entrust
themselves with another life?

No children scream. None catch
fireflies in a jar. Rumsey Playground
lies far too far off the asphalt path
for harried nannies to haul small
charges. *To become the parents*
*we wished we'd had is rare.*
The thought coalesces: a snow-
flake in the muggy air.

# ROBINSON'S PARENTS HAVE COME TO THE CITY FOR A VISIT

What is it about having them around that gets him so wound up?

Parents. Parent(hese)s. Surrounding him & Ann.

How they spent their sunny Sunday:

Gracefully sailing through an array of pratfalls.

He falls to pacing the bedroom.

Bells in the tower of the church next door bellow the hour.

The Our Father pops into his head unbidden; he is not a pray-er.

Hidden from his family, he contemplates his patronym.

Hymns skim the summer air. Robinson's composing a patronymic.

Though his father's name is not Robin—

Though he is not Robin's son—

Robinson is still Robinson.

He could be re-named, but the backstory can't be undone.

Robinson's son's son's son & back & back like a mirror facing a mirror & on & on.

Robinson: the robbing son—what's he taken? What's he done?

He's been feeling lately that if he's not more grateful, he'll lose what he's got.

The paterfamilias—graying old man—doesn't understand him, but is proud nonetheless.

Robinson has no desire to be the pater for any familias.

The loneliness of childhood—shameful condition—

it feels like it will never end & there is no remedy.

# ROBINSON STOOPS ON HIS STOOP

to retrieve the milkman's delivery,
halfway savoring the waking city—
the insomniac neighbor hanging laundry
across the street, newspapers thwacking
the concrete like heartbeats.
                    The usual pyroglazed bottle
now has a tinted label—house, flag, toothy
white fence—that makes him contemplate
the life suburban. This thought disturbs him.
A quaint taste flavors the morning's first
cigarette—dissatisfaction?
          Smoke mixes with his frozen breath.
Robinson tends to forget there are places
other than here. He and his wife could pack up,
start a little family:
          *We would look very much*
*like one bottle of milk, standing alongside*
*ten thousand other bottles of milk.*

## ROBINSON ESCAPES TO THE CAPE FOR INDEPENDENCE DAY

O little-known facts—how Robinson attracts them!

Pilgrims rocked ashore here, before Plymouth Rock.

The word scrimshaw is of unknown origin.

The stock name of the archaic two-lane main road? Route 6A. Really it's Old King's Highway.

Some facts are useless: the paper bag was invented in Dennis.

Some facts are not: Wellfleet's town clock sings out ship's time.

19th century Americans observed only three holidays. The Fourth of July was one.

O witty aperçus—how Robinson accrues them!

Good food is self-made, like a good millionaire.

Don't just do something. Stand there.

It's got to be the weekend somewhere.

Robinson is crisp & perspicuous. His wife stands next to him on the sand.

Democracy could be a lot more sexy if…this one fades in the rockets' red glare.

Ann blushes, runs a hand through his hair.

Robinson looks up, concussed.

Fireworks percuss.

# ROBINSON SENDS A LETTER TO SOMEONE

*Cento III*

For some reason or another I seem to have a car.
It runs;
      though the interior must have been used
exclusively for hauling porcupines & railroad spikes.
Looks a little like an unmade bed in a Bowery fleabag.
Drove down to the Cape—
          Wellfleet—
                Provincetown.
Live here in a state of almost uninterrupted sloth;
occasionally totter over to the piano to play "Someone
to Watch Over Me," or walk across the dunes to swim
& beachcomb, or to the Tennis Club to play ping pong.

Most of the nightclubs are deserted:
        & from the quality of their entertainers,
                well deserve to be.

But the beaches are wonderful. On the bureau:
a huge seashell that looks like Paul Klee had a hand in its design,
an odd cork object, a piece of driftwood shaped like a dolphin,
a stone with a pattern out of Arp, a number of dried starfish...


Feelings of uncertainty & inadequacy keep playing hell with me.

# AT A THURSDAY NIGHT PARTY ON A BOAT IN PROVINCETOWN

a piano rests beneath drinks
& stars. Guests mill at bars

above & belowdecks. Robinson
desires—& tires of—the semi-

constant public performance
required: the chronic flux

& seamy flaunt. A certain
sartorial raffishness. The lurid

math of how drunk to get.
How the devil does anyone

get any work done here?
Would Robinson like to be

the subject of more gossip
or less? Whispers or yawns?

He can't abide boorishness,
but despises boredom.

Manners can get in the way
of a man. Attendees blur

into samizdat versions of
themselves. Perversions

don't get more pronounced,
necessarily—just announced

more loudly: *You'd want me
to treat you like an animal,*

*if you knew how well I like*
*animals.* And *I like a man*

*so tan he's practically ultra-*
*violet.* The host studies

Robinson's hands like
a haruspex; knows he plays

piano, sometimes, at Wuther-
ing Heights. To wuther,

Robinson replies, means to blow
with a dull roaring sound. Lets

himself be prevailed upon
to do the party the honor.

All around, clusters position
themselves for sexual intrigue.

Or not. Robinson's become
master of the faintly deliberate

casual gesture: leaving the tie
around your neck untied.

One rule of attraction? Never
act like you want the thing

you're attracting. Actually,
Robinson's bad at that.

Beneath the refinement,
he's dearly sincere.

Incompletion makes people
want to fill your blanks in.

## DOWN-CAPE, ROBINSON ENCOUNTERS AN OVER-FRIENDLY WAITER

Robinson didn't know, but now
he's been told: *You'll only love oysters*
*from the sea you swam in as a child.*
Thirty-odd years old, Robinson's
all grown up. Late of NYC, he's really
from the late Great Plains, the great
American desert, the sea of grass
that has no real sea. He & his wife—
herself from Wyoming—drove
to Wellfleet anyway to see how
they'd fare with the oysters there.
Tideflats at twilight & the sky alight
with shreds of sunset & boatlights
& oysters in a light brine swimming
on a platter. Wellfleet used to be
known as Port Aux Huitres. Fact
of the matter is, they are ugly creatures:
brackish, smutty, calcified. *Oysters R best*
*to eat in months containing the letter R.*
*Har-dee-har*, says the waiter. *Good thing*
*it's SeptembeR.* Ann is always making
her polite, breathy laugh. Robinson's always
saying yes to inessential requests. She's wearing
a dress she copied from Henri Bendel.
Their table, a still-life: *Oysters, Lemon,*
*& Half-Empty Jug of Wine with Tipsy Wife.*
Robinson doesn't know, but he's been told.
Robinson doubts he'll ever get old.
Their waiter's been reading M.F.K. Fisher:
*an oyster leads a dreadful but exciting life.*
Consider consider consider the oyster.

# AT RACE POINT BEACH, ROBINSON SMOKES TEA

Some things are no longer too huge to explain. Why?

Plain & simple: the planes of sand, planes of the sky, planes of the sea.
Why?

Because: high.

Their friend the painter claims the waves look like ponies in the surf.
Why?

Robinson remains smooth. Ann's a boozy confessor.

*I see my man from far away. Orion is his name.*

She's in love with someone who'll never distress her.

*I blow him a kiss every night. I call him my guy in the sky.*

At this rate, they'll never wake in time to make their orisons.

To swim the cold sea in the cold morning light.

Tonight they are caparisoned. Richly ornamented in fine beachwear.

Tiny lights bob on the water like candles.

Tiny creatures phosphoresce: incandescent benefaction.

Man of action or of contemplation? Robinson inwardly wishes for
more.

But this is an Experience. This is The Life.

His wife becomes spastic. Robinson pleonastic. Too many words.

Every rationalization has its rational side.

They collapse with laughter. What's an ever-after? What are they
after?

The stars in the sky: insignias or asterisks?

Where are the footnotes? Nothing makes sense.

Tiny lights blink out on the waves: dying.

*What can save us?* Robinson asks, exhaling.

*For what kind of reward should we be applying?*

# ROBINSON SENDS A LETTER TO SOMEONE

*Cento IV*

Everyone I know who has been called up
by the draft lately has been rejected—

I went up to Grand Central Palace
& was lovingly placed in classification 4F.

It is difficult to figure out why big
organizations do anything they do.

The people at the top are as bewildered
as the people at the bottom.

(What is psychological classification
72B?; that's what *I'm* in.)

Did I mention to you that *Time* & I
came to a parting of the ways? The arteries

are hardening; there is much worry.
We were ostensibly working a five-day

week; I was always working seven,
& always going to screenings on what

were hopefully referred to as "weekends."
At the sound of the question (from one

of the Senior Editors): "Are you happy
here?" you know your goose is cooked.

I'm going to try to stay away
from a regular job as long as I can, unless

something so tempting that I can't resist
it comes along. Nearing the end. Write.

# ROBINSON IDENTIFIES WITH THE ANIMALS

inside the Bronx Zoo. They too inhabit
an adolescent city: exotic tourism meets
inchoate residency.
                            Chilean flamingos
flex their clipped wings, pinkly. A docile
breeze blows across the "African Plains,"
carrying with it a gamey scent. Robinson
thinks of the park as a life raft
aboard which creatures can survive
the human flood, which even now rushes
up & through the ornate lunettes
of the Memorial Gate,
                            bronze tarnished a light sea-
green, with sculpted effigies of zoo celebrities,
long-deceased: Buster the Galapagos tortoise,
Jimmy the Shoebill stork, Sultan the African lion,
                            displaced as refugees.
The mighty American bison shed, thickly,
a concession to the season. The polar bears
look sickly, splashing in cement pools against
the Indian summer heat.
                            Robinson ducks
into the Primate House, where he regards
the monkeys, their tiny hands so like those
of man. Into the pungent dark, he mutters:
*Will these beasts ever be satisfied*
*with this human architecture?*
*This uncanny surface beneath*
*their canny feet? Will I in my*
*sublet on East 10ᵗʰ Street?*

41

# ROBINSON ON THE ROOFDECK

Standing at the railing in the failing
summer light, Robinson turns his collar
against the clammy air. Sees cars

whizzing across the Brooklyn Bridge
from here. Hears the last party
of the season wheezing to a close.

*Grade-A-O.K. with me,* he says. Stares.
Wires swoop like gulls down to who-knows-where.
Thinks about jumping. Thinks of going home early.

Soon. Alone. Then someone sees him—

drunk...
        making eye contact...
                swoon.

There's something sexy in desolation.

## ROBINSON & THE WORD

Natty dresser, that
Robinson's window
shopping. Just lost
his job; he's not
stopping anywhere.
Staring at finery
behind plate glass,
about to pass a florist's
when he sees the sign:
Consider the Lilies,
so he does: *how they
grow; they toil not,
neither do they spin.*
Gives him the willies.
As literature, it's pretty,
but those who swear
by it seem unstable
as three-legged tables.
Robinson prefers
to try to be good
for goodness's own
sake, not for a stake
in impending reward.
*But ah me of little faith—
being good is hard,*
he sighs to the painted
board. Goes inside,
buys some lilies
for Ann. Dangling
from his gloved
right hand, their
waxen blooms bang
at his knees. *I will
never be arrayed
like one of these.*

# ROBINSON SENDS A LETTER TO SOMEONE

*Cento V*

"When in doubt, do nothing."
                    —Marcus Aurelius.
To do it week after week, & keep one's sanity,
is quite a trick.
                    I am in doubt.
Cocktail parties with martinis & uninteresting guests—
nobody much gives a damn whether you write
or take dope or read the *American Magazine*.
                              I play things like
"What Is This Thing Called Love?" & "St. Louis Blues"
on the Steinway concert grand in the music room.
                              I wish awfully that you
would come back to N.Y. for a while.
Last night,
        found an album of Bix Beiderbecke
records buried among Bach & Shostakovich.
                              All were dutifully played.
Late in the evening, sitting out in the hallway,
quite alone, on the cooling radiator, head in hands.
So much to say, & as you once said:
        some things just don't get into letters.

## ROBINSON CAN'T READ

whole books anymore.
       Anything longer than half a page
    & the words swim
like small, fierce fish before his eyes. He blames
    the jumpy pace of the age
& his own nerves, fraying like electrical cord.
       Still he trawls
the open stalls of Books 'N Things
      & all the secondhand sellers
lining Fourth Ave.    just to see what they have:
*Les Fleurs du Mal*    *The Art of the Insane*
*The Man Who Watched Trains Go By*
    & other titles he already owns.
    He buys a crumbly copy
of *Death's Jest-Book* by Thomas L. Beddoes.
    As for the rest?
    Useless, desperate crap,
stuff he could never force himself to read,
    even back when he still could:
*Divorce: the Wreck of Marriage* &
    *Think & Grow Rich*
& *How to Sell Your Way Through Life.*
    Yet he can't stop looking:
    *Just for Two:*
*a handbook of cookery for the small household*
    & he hasn't a clue as to why.
A bowlegged bald man catches his eye—
    he's snatching up the paperback of
    *Love Without Fear*
& for a second, Robinson's jealous.
    Then he's paralyzed again,
by the usual phantom—
      so many books,
      so short a life,
& so many poor fools wasting their time.
Silly imperative: *Love Without Fear.*
    What's ever so clear.

# ROBINSON SENDS A LETTER TO SOMEONE

*Cento VI*

Midafternoon:
                    I come away
from the window & the rooftops
& turn the knob on the radio—
          a thin line cutting
across rows of numbers.
I would like to hear, say,
Jelly Roll playing "The Crave,"
                    but will settle
for a Lee Wiley record.
                              Except
for a station on which a voice
          not easily distinguishable
from Miss Margaret Truman's
          is singing "At Dawning"
& another on which "light classics"
by a feeble string group emerge
     oppressively distinct,
all the others are playing
     record       after     record
     by big dance bands:
Claude Thornhill,
               Kay Kyser,
                         Tex Beneke,
               Charlie Spivak
Vaughn Monroe.
    Corruption & decay.
I switch off the radio,
          go
into the other room,
          pour myself
                    a drink.

# ROBINSON HAS FALLEN OUT OF LOVE

with this city: less place than metaphor—
       but what for, really?
Down residential streets,
his two-tone wingtips crunch
through leaves, past rowhouses—
warm, low, curled in on themselves
like sleeping cats.
            No, like shadowboxes.
The shades of some are drawn like scrims
exposing only silhouettes. No one sees him.
Through lit windows, Robinson studies
their setpieces: fireplaces & radios,
horsehair sofas, overstuffed ottomans
& dinner dishes. A far-sighted man
surrounded by bookcases reads Cervantes,
like his father did, through a pair of pince-nez.

Robinson hears the yells of couples fighting,
smells the smells of—potroast?—cooking,
looking        looking        looking
until he's cold under the husk of his topcoat.

A man—thinning hair—& a woman—heavy calves—
dance in their kitchen, in the gathering gloom,
laugh as they knock into the phonograph playing
"The Blue Room." Robinson sees she's pregnant.

*Things will never be the same*, he says.
*Fine. But will they ever get better?*
The face of H.—childhood friend—flickers
through his mind. A little nostalgia fits
like a warm sweater this time of year.

# ROBINSON SUFFERS THE WINTER SOLSTICE

Longest night of the year.
Long night of the heart,
the throat, the nose, the lungs.
Robinson's sick.
Ann sleeps beside
him, snuffling slightly,
numb with Valium.
Frost limns their loft's
innumerable windows,
rendering them semi-
opaque, small skating rinks
beyond which flakes, filthy
as pigeons, slither past.
Robinson contemplates
burning their books
for heat. Treats himself
to a nightcap instead,
speaks into the headless
neck of the bottle:
*you are my pharmakon,*
*my medicine, my poison.*
The city sinks under snow.
The dark lumbers on.

# ROBINSON SENDS A LETTER TO SOMEONE

*Cento VII*

"The art of letter-writing is a lost art."
      —Elizabeth Barrett Browning,
or was it Irita Van Doren?
      We live in confusing times.

People here have quieted down
      considerably since the fall;
whether it indicates a fatalistic state of mind
      or the quiet before the storm
I don't know and don't much like to think about.

A thriving business is being done in *God Bless America* signs:

*God Bless America* buttons
      (for gentleman's lapel),
    *God Bless America* recordings
      (by Kate Smith),
and *God Bless America* banners
      (liquor stores are biggest purchasers of these,
          strangely).

There is also a song out (which you surely have heard)
      called I AM AN AMERICAN
          (and proud of my liber-tee).

The Gallup poll says a substantial majority of citizens
      favor an American fascism—
The administration must be supported
      in everything they do.
I guess I'll get my GOD BLESS AMERICA banner out,
and parade around a few blocks while I hum on my old kazoo.

We live in confusing times. An idiot wind is blowing;
the conscience dies. I hope this finds you still out of the army...
What a gloomy communication! Where will it all end?

though he'll readily admit: he's no outdoorsman.
Natural beauty can floor him. Then? Boredom.

Yet skating elates. Skating exhilarates. Invigorates,
sans irony, his childhood memory: iron skates

made in his grandfather's factory. Racing
across the ice, Robinson traces ampersands.

His kid-self called his parents *John & Sarah*, not
*Mom & Dad*, trolled through Victrola records,

lolled across the dial for radio shows from far away:
Chicago. Cincinnati. Avoided the lock- & gun-

smith business of his family. He gets to the end
of the rink & spins. His motto in the yearbook:

*A little nonsense now & then is relished by the best of men.*
Robinson imagines a fight inside him: anomie

v. bonhomie, each with a skate blade—no,
a pistol. Cruel smile v. nice. Each taking twenty

paces then facing off. A duel! Who'll win?
Beneath the gilded statue of Prometheus

recumbent, bringing light to man, Robinson
tries to remain upright, a Sunday school verse

for adversity refusing to leave his head:
*If you fall, don't cry. Give a merry laugh instead!*

# ROBINSON ENDS UP ATTENDING MASS AT XMAS

Aria. Luminaria. *Ave Maria*!

All babies are pretty when lit from above.

This evening's service is the Children's Pageant.

Robinson's aberrant for not having any.

Aloof & brooding: hedonist or anhedonist?

He rides the death drive. Steers clear of little ones.

Queer & queerer.

But Robinson doesn't much care what you've heard.

Robinson's mother never let him write Xmas: *It's like you're Xing out Jesus.*

They're not even Catholic.

Post-college, post-Christ—how to believe now that he's educated?

The pastor keeps the homily short for the families.

Something something *Those who dwelt in the land of deep darkness.*

Something something about *light,* then *Silent Night* in German.

The biggest damper on holiday cheer is adulthood.

Robinson fakes like he has somewhere to go.

Snow cloaks the city: brittle. The thin layer of ice on top of a drink.

St. for *street* or St. for *saint*?

*Xmas lights on the fire escape make escaping fires more festive.*

The quip slips from his lips, though no one is listening.

Robinson stumbles up the sidewalk, humble as a manger.

# AFTER THE HOLIDAY

Dead tree after dead tree,
white curb after curb curbs

the vigor of the season,
Robinson reasons. January,

emissary of the year to come,
shines dull & dumb so far.

*Who do others think you are?*
Robinson wheedles, kicking

the needles of the pine re-
pining at his feet, reminding

him of the "Tree Menagerie"
on the grounds surrounding

his first college in Crete,
Nebraska, branches & leaves

replete with shapes: animal
& abstract. How to react

to the gothic middle west? To
the middle west grotesque?

The trees were not evergreen.
What did they mean & to whom

did they speak? Best to forget.
It hurts to think of them, hurts

to think of sly sex perverts—
bachelor professors, sweaty text-

book reps—who stepped up
to him then. Was it his communism,

frilly & pink? Was it his eyes,
sad & deep? The whys & where-

fores interest him less now, but
the roots tap at his soul, sole

proprietor of his parents' love.
Darling of their hearts, land-

locked in the heartland, posed
for Baby's First Christmas

in a tiny sailor suit. The halls:
decked. The walls: flecked

with light. An ornament falling
from the Scotch pine behind

him: out of focus, a cute
Icarus arcing through a life

of sub-normal calm. What
has changed since then?

Here, he is hailed, hailed,
hailed again—*Hello, sailor!*

Why this appeal? It doesn't
feel like it belongs to him.

Still, he'd like to keep it, lock
it up in a locket like a lock

of hair where it won't cause
worry. Sometimes he thinks

of himself, dark as a pocket,
scattered to the wind.

He should hurry home.
Yet even when hidden,

Robinson stands out. Gold
flashing at the back of a mouth.

## ROBINSON & ANN AGREE

they have to leave the East Coast.
Side by side they lay in bed.

Stare at the crack in their sublet's
ceiling . It appears to leer back.

Reduced to penury, they call
the place a slumlet. This lack

of resources oppresses. Renders
them brainless as Ann's dress-

maker's dummy. Hints still present
themselves, though, of who they

were long ago, when they got
married in Denver. *Kaleradoe,*

they say, like natives, to make
themselves laugh. Neither

believed in god then, either,
but as a nod to their parents,

they thought it best to make each
other honest. Both are allergic

to sentiment. Sometimes they
play a game to get time to go

faster: if we were in a story, what
would be the genre? "There's been

a wedding," says Ann, "but will
there be a death?" Robinson

thinks, *Of course there will.* "This
is the pace that kills," says Ann.

# ROBINSON SENDS A LETTER TO SOMEONE

*Cento VIII*

"A letter," says Laura Riding, "must be composed
in leisure. Its wrongness must have the authoritative
formality of a premeditated crime. A letter written
because its author could not help writing it
is an act of insanity."

I find myself becoming more & more anti-social:
it is an ordeal to get myself out of the house
& there are fewer & fewer people I care about seeing.
It may be the end of New York as a romantic idea.

"The mails are full of helpless insanity."

I would like to live in a warm place by the ocean
& weave baskets or split kindling wood.
I've done an enormous number of paintings since
you were here, but not many of them are very good.

Every so often
I take a teaspoonful
of some evil-looking black medicine.

I worry about how to relax. The doctor couldn't tell me.
So here we are with our Flents,
                    our frayed nerves,
                        our new Hans Knoll furniture,
none too securely held up by floors that look as though
a herd of large, solid-hoof herbivorous animals
had once used them for hourly stampedes.

People in general here are behaving
                        with greater wackiness
than ever before in my experience. Outside
in the courtyard, a man in a gray hat & gray topcoat
has been standing for a long time now
                        making little marks
on a piece of paper.          A map?          Maybe so.

He keeps looking in the windows.
Do you think this means anything? No more paper. Write.

# ROBINS MIGHT LAND ON A STATUE OF ROBINSON

if he ever gave the city
    any reason to build one.
        Past ponderous bronzes

of Beethoven, Burns, & a stern
    metal man whose identity he's
        unsure of, Robinson leans

almost into the Untermeyer Fountain,
    yearns to shed the sense he'll die
        before his parents.

American elm seeds drift down
    like confetti as he thinks
        of posterity.

If he expects to leave any sort
    of legacy, he'll have to leave
        this leaden city.

Breeze across the water scatters his
    reflection. Mirrors, like monuments,
        have no real memory.

## WHAT DOES HE WANT? THE FUTURE! WHEN DOES HE WANT IT? NOW!

Driving by a driving range
on their way out of town,

Robinson sees golf balls
knocked from tees—

clocked through atmosphere.
*Trylon*, he thinks. *Perisphere*.

*1939 New York World's Fair.*
He was there. He was there.

In the letter he carefully wrote
to his friend in the Army,

he rolled his hand-written eyes:
*they think mankind can rise*

*to the firmament.* Now he writes:
*razed & scrapped for World War*

*armaments.* The world of tomorrow?
Here to stay. Rumbling away

from NYC, Robinson passes
the rubble of Democracity.

In spite of himself, he misses
that scene. The Aquacade.

The Helicline. The sweet belief—
in incline, not decline—that he

wanted to have, but even then
couldn't find. What could have

remained a national treasure, now

seems the last full measure

of obscene sarcasm. The war
was a chasm they were suspended

above. What will become
of them on the other side?

Memory is corrupt. Infinitely
corruptible. But he remembers:

*they sold fun & we bought it. We
bought it.* Xerox. Air conditioning.

RCA TV. German jet planes.
Kodachrome & color home

movies. Plexiglas. Lucite.
No point trying to fight it.

II.

# AT A MOTEL IN THE SHADOW OF A SAD RIVER CITY

Robinson resents Ann's placid sleep.

A flaccid inanity keeps him awake:

*Now here* is *nowhere.*

None of their East Coast friends would know where they are.
Ohiowa? No. Just Ohio.

Procter & Gamble, soap & candles.

Robinson wonders: *have we made a mistake?*

Ann ordered a slice of red velvet cake for dinner; they are far enough
South.

Blood-colored food gives Robinson the creeps.

Light slits in through the blinds, & Robinson is reminded of the day's
near-miss:

Columbia Parkway, with its dead man's curve—

the asphalt jungle, New Deal art deco—

almost bungled the turn, killed them both.

The busted boomtown used to be known as the Queen of the West.

Ann's always been as aware as he is of the nightmare—

what happens next & what is left?

Either she's forgotten or she doesn't care.

Pallid. Whipsawed. Robinson needs to rest.

But the more he thinks so, the more his brain goes—

disloyal engine, machining through the ether.

## ROBINSON TEARS PAGES FROM *THE RAND MCNALLY ROAD ATLAS*

one for each state they've driven through so far.
    Keeps the maps on the black upholstered seat
        of their car because Maine, for instance,
            has been printed on the back of Maryland.

The jagged eastern half of the continental U.S.
    shows through three-quarters worth of Alabama,
        &—held to the light—Mexico looks like
            one of Canada's Atlantic Provinces.

Eyeing the other poor saps in their rolling coffins,
    Robinson's almost forgotten why they left, so he stops.
        Beneath the picnic shelter of an Iowa rest area,
            Robinson & Ann consult atlas-as-medical text:

vein-blue State Routes, red Principal Highways,
    thin pink capillaries of unpaved road.
        They & their fellow motorists are honed
            straight razors, nicking the land.

Over a tinny speaker, the AM station squawks
    the approach of an electrical storm before the signal dissolves
        like salt in water. Their cat, Daughter, hollers
            & the fat, smooth air seems ready to burst.

# ANN INSISTS ON READING THE BURMA-SHAVE ADS OUT LOUD

I.

*Modern man*

    *Spreads it on*

        *Pats it in*

            *Shaves it off*

                *See him grin*

                    *Burma-Shave*

                        II.

                  *A peach looks good*

              *With lots*

        *Of fuzz*

        *But man's no peach*

      *And never wuz*

   *Burma-Shave*

III.

*Other days—*

   *Other ways.*

      *Nowadays*

         *Burma-Shave*

            IV.

         *Aid the blade*

*Burma-Shave*

# REST AREAS MAKE HIM RESTLESS

so Robinson pees quickly into the sick-smelling
urinal. These places may be the most democratic
in the country—uniform, filthy, their users
there for one purpose only
                              (unless they're perverts).
Shoes slipping against the grouty floor,
he pictures his car, unmoored from its spot,
sailing from the lot without him or Ann.
Each driver captains a private ship,
each roadside stop's a little Atlantis,
possibly vanished should they pass again.
And Robinson?
          *Why, I'm the Flying Dutchman*
*of course.*              *Homeless, hurtling*
*West*              *West*              *West*
*along an infinite course, away from New York,*
*nearing the port of impending divorce.*
                              Robinson hoists
his zipper like an anchor, buttons up, shoves off.

## ROBINSON'S CAR IS NOTHING LIKE A PRAIRIE SCHOONER

yet he & Ann schoon the prairie.
His parents moved to Orlando,

so this stop in Beatrice is as
unnecessary as the town itself.

Surrounding farms rot.
Lack things bought, once,

from his father's company:
window-hinges, trellises, railings.

Father wooed Mother mostly
through mailings to live as help-

mate to the scion of a business
in the Cornhusker State

that began by manufacturing
actual cornhuskers.

Robinson love-hated it when
his father tried the same way

to win him to the family fold:
to convince him to grow old

in a wholesome place, writing
letters on stationery from hotels

in Middle Western towns
already fading, but unerasable—

errors in a ledger, terribly kept.
Father even took Son with him

to some of the less depressing:
Robinson saw his first talkie

in the Twin Cities. It was fun
& he wrote a little review

his father had published
in the Beatrice *Daily Sun*.

The Big Blue River used to
shiver with prosperity.

He & Ann walk down
the bank. The river is not

blue but brown & you couldn't
drown in it if you wanted to,

dry as the piece of creeping
gown his mother saved

& pinned to his baby book.
Looking to the skies, they see

no birds. Too hot. Robinson
craves the grace of rainy-day

games, but there seem to be
no more rainy days.

V.

*Every second*

    *Without fail*

        *Some store*

            *Rings up*

                *Another sale*

                    *Burma-Shave*

VI.

                  *Avoid the store*

              *Which claims*

          *You should*

        *Buy something else*

    *That's just as good*

*Burma-Shave*

# VII.

*Don't take*

    *A curve*

        *At 60 per*

            *We hate to lose*

                *A customer*

                    *Burma-Shave*

# OVER A THOUSAND MILES FROM NEW YORK CITY

& Ann is still annoyed Robinson wouldn't stop for her forgotten
cookbooks.

Robinson's almost never not annoyed, though that's been subsiding.

Arriving in Lincoln in time for a death—a funeral procession
processes their path.

The streets near campus are chalky with dust.

This is where they met, in line for class pictures—names chalked in
their respective handwritings.

Robinson pays attention best when he's ignoring something else.

*Touch a button when you see a hearse*, Ann mutters, brushing his cuff—
more stuff her mother taught her, growing up in Wyoming.

He neglects the present by thinking of the past—

juvenilia & miscellany & always always the handsome dress.

The assignments remain long, Robinson suspects, the nights
maddening on dormitory beds.

Who is still around, who in the cemetery?

Ann is wary; a year younger, she looks much older.

Their roadster slinks by the house of the sorority she pledged & her
voice grows edgy.

*Hold on now*, he tells her, *this isn't scary.*

They're at the university to visit a former professor, & when they do?

He wears the same double-breasted suit of robinseggblue & still
professes all he used to profess.

Robinson confesses they don't know what they'll do when they reach the West Coast.

The professor will regret not offering him a job, though Robinson clearly hates Nebraska.

*Wander the beach collecting driftwood to shellac & sell to tourists, I guess.*

Ever the smart aleck.

Last night, in his dream, Robinson invented a system for processing doubt; when he awoke, he couldn't remember how.

# ROBINSON SENDS A LETTER TO SOMEONE

*Cento IX*

Meant to write to you before this—
I always experience horrible agony
      (Oh lost! Lost!)
thrust into a new environment.
Tremendously difficult trying to make the adjustment:
the damned hurry,
         the noise,
              the goddamned lights
enjoining you to mobilize your car chew Ex-lax
& keep regular dine & dance without overcharge.
Was around San Francisco many years ago & loved it—
      full of a sort of dim & woozy good will.
New York got to be too much of a struggle, at least for me,
& one that availeth close to naught.
                  Mostly got tired
of all the dirt & darkness, & getting burned pieces
of the *Mirror* in my left eye everytime I went out
& seeing so many people turning sad &/or crazy.
I'd like to see yr. baby, but can wait until the pulverized-
spinach-spitting stage abates.
            My parents are going through a similar stage
of the uprooting process that you write of yr. own parents.
Mine have sold the house & are clearing out for Orlando.
They have so much vigor & endurance & elation over travel
that I feel, by comparison, like Tiresias around them.
Ann sends her best;
        congratulations on your promotion;
                let us hear from you often.

# ROBINSON KEEPS A TRAVEL JOURNAL IN PALIMPSEST

writing first across, then down the cramped page,
in a tight, black grid of negligible legibility.

Chronicles his trip taking candid snapshots,
with an Argus C3 he picked up at a pawn shop:

"Blonde Couple Fighting in Cherry-red Ragtop,"
"Trucker Sleeping at Rest-stop, Cap Over Face,"

"Toughs Peeling Out of Filling Station, Bill Unpaid."
Can't stop collecting scrapbook ephemera:

sugar packets bearing logos of roadside eateries,
pamphlets for Wonder Spots & OK Kampgrounds,

a Gideon's New Testament from a Best Western
Starlite Village. Sometimes, he envisions a single,

celebratory act: throwing everything away
with his cigarette butts & Styrofoam cups—

ticker-tape in a roadside garbage drum,
having come so far without leaving a trace,

but he can't. There's still as much of yesterday
as there is of tomorrow in all he does today.

# VIII.

*Past*

    *Schoolhouses*

        *Take it slow*

            *Let the little*

                *Shavers grow*

                    *Burma-Shave*

# IX.

        *Here's*

      *A good deed*

    *For a scout*

   *Tell your dad*

  *All about*

*Burma-Shave*

X.

*Mom and Pop*

*Are feeling gay*

*Baby said*

*As plain*

*As day*

*Burma-Shave*

# ROBINSON BUYS A SOUVENIR POSTCARD

of a lonesome man buying a postcard
of a lonesome man buying a postcard
of a lonesome man buying a postcard
of a lonesome man buying a postcard

of a lonesome man buying a postcard
of a lonesome man buying a postcard
of a lonesome man buying a postcard
of a lonesome man buying a postcard

of a lonesome man buying a postcard
of a lonesome man buying a postcard
of a lonesome man buying a postcard
of a lonesome man buying a postcard

of a lonesome man buying a postcard
of a lonesome man buying a postcard

XII.

*At school zones*

*Heed instructions!*

*Protect*

*Our little*

*Tax deductions*

*Burma-Shave*

XIII.

*If these*

*Signs blur*

*And bounce around*

*You'd better park*

*And walk to town*

*Burma-Shave*

XIV.

*Sleep in a chair*

    *Nothing to lose*

        *But a nap*

            *At the wheel*

                *Is a permanent snooze*

                    *Burma-Shave*

# SIXTEEN DAYS IN A LINCOLN ROADSTER

& here they are: the left-most coast.

The Village of Our Lady, the Queen of the Angels, on the Porciúncula River.

Easier, he admits, just to say L.A.

Plainly not alluvial, no longer a floodplain, the climate seems wild, spooky in its mildness.

Annexations & consolidations, grandiloquence & excess.

Ann lived here after they graduated—*Nebraska has given you all she has to offer*, said the commencement speaker.

Oil, orange juice, the sperm of movie stars.

Craning his neck at a variety of angles, Robinson sees no angels.

Less couple-in-a-car, more leaf-blown-about-on-the-earth-by-the-winds, they decide to crash at the Portal Motor Hotel—

a Motel, got it, but a portal to what?

They will go out at night: clarinets & trumpets—a maze of jazz.

Bred to earn his daily bread, Robinson once dropped out of vocational psych.

The motto of the city: augment augment augment.

Bored by pioneers, Robinson tries to be pioneering.

Prospector without prospects, or potentially too many?

Cement cement cement buries all trace of the old enterprise of gold.

III.

# ROBINSON SENDS A LETTER TO SOMEONE

*Cento X*

California seems to debase itself
less frenetically than the East Coast.
At least my central nervous system
has responded to it rather nicely.

We were sort of at loose ends for a time:
waiting around for an apartment
at the above address to become available.
It *was* to have been ready for us around the 1st,
but a strike of tile-layers screwed things up
but good. Perhaps a little detail would not be
out of order: a large L-shaped living room,
a bedroom, kitchen, bath & a room I can use
as a studio, a few steps from a beach
on the bay, surrounded by eucalyptus trees,
& a half-hour drive from downtown SF.

—Then our furniture came, intact,
scarcely anything broken, & that meant
a couple of days off for arranging,
cleaning, wood-creaming, sandpapering.

Never once have I caught myself
humming "Give My Regards to Broadway,"
& it is an unconfined joy not to walk
ankle-deep in NY's minglement of snow,
slush, banana skins, burned newspapers
& carbon bi-products of the Mssrs. Edison,
not to experience that city's capacity
for Angst,
  not to mention
    not to mention
      not to mention
        not to mention…

# SETTING UP HOUSEKEEPING IN SAN FRANCISCO,

the new place comes with a different cast of light,

some Western privacy,

& a set of cats

& so Daughter is joined by Lonesome & Pulque.

Ann doesn't care much one way or the other about pets,

but Robinson adores the triumvirate:

their inveterate roaming,

their courtly disdain,

their seeming transported from a remote time of great romantic cachet.

Though he knows he should attempt aloofness, Robinson gets attached.

He studies, as such, their many flawed teachings:

how to act thankless as a minor god,

how to sulk like you mean it,

how to be uncontained by rooms.

Their first cat, Flowerface, fell off the roof back in Denver.

When Ann wrote to tell him, he responded with laughter, though after, he acknowledged it very unfunny.

How these cats meow: fulsome.

How they create a masterly reverberation.

How they hold themselves apart.

## INSIDE THE BUNGALOW HOUSE

with the wide front porch—

which they do not own, but rent—

Ann drinks alone. During the day. For no particular reason.

Robinson tends to pretend this happens only sometimes.

Keeps giving them occasions—to entertain & be entertained.

Inviting new acquaintances over has always been his métier.

Sometimes, Robinson can keep looking forward to things that have
already happened.

He can be petulant, too, sometimes. Sometimes unbiddable.

& words get caught, unforgettable, sometimes in his head:

the rhyme stitched on the britches of the Raggedy Andy

left behind the sofa the other evening by the child of a friend:

*Annie, do you love me or do you not?*

*You told me once, but I forgot.*

The best way to deal with not getting what you want

is sometimes to knock off wanting it.

# THEIR NEW APARTMENT CAME WITH A GARDEN

though Robinson has no clue
how to make it do anything.

Sun & 65 heavy semi-humid
degrees—Robinson agrees

with their new climate.
Surveys the scene. The plot.

The obscenely named botany:
Calendula. Convolvulus.

A kind of pretty that's
always seemed unreal:

silk flowers, fake birds, cakes
of scent. Ann's taken the car.

Part-time secretarial. *Off
to earn our daily gin,* she said,

skidding down the drive.
Would have been cute, if

she'd been kidding. The marigolds
turn with the sun. Robinson

picks one. The reverse
of a *memento mori* must be

a *carpe diem*. His head
thrums. A bumblebee

generates a molecular
hurricane. The rays create

a scorching efflorescence
& the land seems a bad

dream gone really bad.
If he keeps sleep-

walking like this, there's
going to be an accident.

## ROBINSON HATES HOW HE SOMETIMES BEHAVES

How he acts in such a way now
that he can almost hear them later:

*we'd always seen it coming.*
*That Robinson—always saying*
*he was fine, like he wanted us*
*to believe him, but also like he*
*wanted us to see, wanted us*
*to ask why he sometimes seemed*
*smooth as a mustachioed actor,*
*other times like he was staging*
*some tell-tale gesture—*

a man wearing a mask
& pointing to the mask.

# 'TIS THE SEASON TO SUBMIT

to a superior power, but
Robinson submits he's inferior

at that. Christmas in California
contradicts past Christmases—

the sunny exteriors, equable,
serene. The neighbors

polishing their automobiles,
swollen & gleaming like not-

so-latent fantasies. Of carols
played at *tempo di schitzi*

& Ann doing needlepoint
on small pillowcases: tiny

Matisses perfect for gift-
giving. 'Tis the season to give

as good as one's getting.
Of winter rains coming, but

not here yet. Of sending
handmade cards to distant

friends, signed "Sigmund Claus"
with cutout Coca Cola Santas:

*Noel! Here's wishing you an oral*
*Christmas & an anal New Year.*

Of a pamphlet in the mail asking
*Has God Been Insulted Here?*

Of driving around to look
at the lights & finding whole

districts to be demolished
for superhighways—going,

going, woebegone.  Of torpor
bulging, of being unable

to budge. Of receiving letters
that leverage inevitable

comparisons.  Of asking
*When will I learn—& really*

*believe—that other people's*
*success does not mean I am*

*not succeeding?* Of saying
*Wait—don't answer that.*

# ROBINSON SENDS A LETTER TO SOMEONE

*Cento XI*

We came out here almost two years ago
& are glad we did.
        By the winter of 1949-1950
I would have settled for Atchison
           or Lone Pine, Ark.,
it had gotten that unappetizing.
I have the best damned place to work
in I've ever had—a moderate-sized room
at the back of the house, with a crummy
floor that I don't mind dripping paint
onto & good space & light.

The grim facts must be faced:
        we like it out here enormously
& our all too infrequent throbbings
of nostalgia, so far as the East,
relate to folks such as you & Mary
& not to the locus or its geist.

One afternoon Tony & I climbed down
a mountain back of their house to the ocean
& saw a sealion swimming & a huge rock
covered with cormorants, all in profile
& looking like society ladies in black
at a swank opening.

        Various vistas opening up here.

Hope all goes well & that the storm
           spared you both.
I wish you all the best with your marriage.
Ann sends her love. Write soon.

# ROBINSON RECALLS HIS FIRST YEAR OF MARRIAGE

She used to walk through the house, skirt rustling
like rain. How was he to know she'd end up drunk—

face puffed like a corpse in a lake? That they'd grow
as capable of savagery as they used to be of grace?

Long before the strain of life on the coasts, they
toasted each other after work at night, getting tight

together on gin & 7 Up. When it got too late
for her to read, or him to type, they'd fall asleep,

& share the same dreams, & sometimes wake up
in the middle of a thunderstorm. It would seem

as though the walls all had open eyes, & that the rain
could sing, & love would ring through the room.

Now, when they scream at each other like the world
might end, that's the time he most likes to remember:

twin hearts, full, in the American heartland.
Whenever they stop shouting, & she's back

to tugging on his sleeve, begging him to tell her
where he's hidden her bottles, Robinson

searches her eyes for their old, smart gleam:
that sparkle like a diamond atop another diamond.

# ROBINSON COMBS BAKER BEACH NEAR FORT POINT

long after the shore has been emptied of sun-bathers,
when only teenaged hoodlums & fumbling lovers
remain around the masonry & the blasted white cliff

where artillerymen stood guard for a war that never came.
Roaming the sand, he's searching for glass bottles,
collecting empties in a sack at his side. He breaks
them against the rocks as if christening a ship,

casts blue, brown, & green shards as far as he can
out into the tide. Listens to them splash. Imagines
them like memory: sharp at first—edgy. But polished
eventually—smooth & melancholy. He drinks

from his flask. Asks unaccountable questions
of seagulls sleeping on posts & granite: "How is it
that I've never found a single message? Or a map?"

# IN THE ONLY SELF-PORTRAIT

he'll ever paint,
                Robinson despairs
of ever getting the likeness right:
face white as a saint,
         hair dark as a cave,
brown eyes fixed, alight,
           bright as magnesium—
dips his favorite sable
into a kidney-shaped blob
         of Red Gold Lake
bled from a crumpled lead tube
         of Old Holland paint—
scores his own throat
              with a dotted line
labeled
        *Please*        *CutHere.*
Studies the results in the shaving mirror.
        Reaches for the turpentine.

# ROBINSON PREPARES HIMSELF

a TV dinner, though he owns no TV,
& wouldn't watch it if he did,
                              staring instead
out the window toward the bridge,
                              hidden
now in mist, but there all the same.
                              His wife's
gone again, maybe this time for good,
locked away in a ward at Langley Porter.
                              KPFA
plays on the kitchen radio,
                              & the Pall Mall
in the ashtray—unfiltered, slow—smokes itself.
The oven timer dings & Robinson jumps,
alarming the cat at his feet.
                              Peeling
the wrinkled foil back with a flick
of his finely-cuffed wrist, he reveals
turkey awash in gelatinous gravy,
          whipped sweet potatoes,
                    & crumpled peas:
          buttered, greenish-gray.
Steam rises from the aluminum tray,
hot as breath
                    from a sleeping body,
damp as the fog settling over the Bay,
          warm & moist in his face,
                         in his mouth
          as he opens it to say:
*This supper, this place, this life, this ring
are mere contingencies, not to be confused
          in any way with real things.*

# ROBINSON SENDS A LETTER TO SOMEONE

*Cento XII*

Ann & I are separating: that is one item.*
I'm a little blank about it at the moment.
Over the 4th of July weekend
      she went completely paranoid—
drank continuously, & I was unable
to get any psychiatric help, since
all the boys & girls were off at the seashore
& the mountains for that lovely weekend.
                Two nights a nice MD
next door shot her full of sodium amytal,
& occasionally she would have a lucid moment.
Most of the time she was not sure who she was,
who I was & there was a very deep certainty
on her part that FBI men were outside the house.
      Well, that ain't the half of it;
finally, on Tuesday morning I got hold
of one of the few psychiatrists around here
of any real help on such cases & she agreed
to sign herself in
              at Langley Porter Clinic.
She improved greatly there, but left against advice
after three weeks.
      She has agreed to a divorce,
& I hope she will be all right. We were married
for sixteen years & a lot of it was not so good.
It's too bad that her life could not have been one long
summer on the cape, because she was at her best then.
      I incline toward the Scott Fitzgerald
theory of emotional exhaustion, that one
has only so large an account to draw on,
& once you've drawn on it,
              that's all there is.

*Please say nothing of this.

# ROBINSON IS TAKING A BREAK FROM PAINTING

because he can't keep drawing straight lines
with a crooked heart. Colors haven't looked

the same since he & Ann parted ways
& art never was his first love anyway.

Plans for expressing abstractions
have become obnoxious, literal:

topographical maps of faint white sand
where she last left her sandals to dry,

wrinkles in the bedsheets where
she used to lie like an odalisque.

A monochromatic series in the harshest
light: ash from her last cigarettes

in the tray he can't quite bring himself
to empty, the premature lightening

of her thick dark hair. The sun rises gray
this morning over Dana Street, revealing

a landscape of threats & darkness.
*When I picture my future, I see a blank*

*white wall. That's all,* he says
aloud to no one in particular.

# ROBINSON WRESTLES WITH THAT OLD DESPAIR

Aware that to be a functional human being means
to deny death, but having lately suffered a loss

of interest in that fact, Robinson has taken to staying
inside—curtains drawn, phone off the hook.

Won't answer the door, won't even look through
the peephole. Familiar faces have gone filmy in his mind—

the kind of photo the lab gives refunds for. Robinson
has moved; told his lawyer—but not Ann—where.

Rests now, quietly, in his favorite chair, unsure
what's required to snap himself out of it. Thinks

he sees a light in the closet that would be hers,
were he & she still sharing, but when he gets up

to check, the bulb is cold. It's dark as his heart
in there, & as empty, save an ugly pair of slacks

she didn't want to keep, & near to the ground
a smell he can't identify. He lies down for a bit

to see if it won't come to him. It won't.
He can't recall what he's supposed to be

seeking, though he knows that this is not quite
the time to quit; he'd better get back to it.

# ROBINSON'S SEPARATED, NOT DIVORCED

He keeps his affairs sort of secret.

He's taken to sleeping with a small brunette.

Glamour packs a wallop.

Eros has a way.

*You probably should get what you want (& be sufficiently scared about it)*

is what she said the first time they went to bed together.

So does Thanatos.

Robinson stares at the side of her face. Wants to declare:

*Adultery does not come from the Latin a-dolescere. To grow up. To mature. To adult.*

Robinson's never felt older.

There will be fault. There will be guilt.

Her camisole's wilted over the back of a chair

& all the ice has melted from the whiskey on the table.

She says *I hope hell is half this fun.*

Adultery comes from *ad-ulterare. To corrupt.*

Robinson says *I already feel fairly far from God's love.*

She interrupts to suck his cock.

Abrupt abrupt.

Robinson's being ridiculous.

Perhaps it's in silence that the best work is done.

He wonders if he will ever remember how it feels to be loved—

if it comes back, it comes back, it comes back. If it comes.

# ROBINSON SETS HIS HOUSE IN ORDER

Literally, unfortunately.
      Not metaphorically.

His marriage, it seems, is finally over
complete with an attorney & papers
to be signed next week.

*just as well*      *just as well*      *just as well*

he keeps telling himself, but he feels—
& his new place looks—like hell.
                    So
in chinos & a white Oxford shirt with rolled-up sleeves,
can of bleach in one hand, tumblerful of ice & whiskey
      at the ready,

            Robinson cleans
     & cleans
& cleans
     & cleans
'til—if nothing else—

      his toilet shimmers,
      & his kitchen beams.

## FASTIDIOUS AS HE IS,

Robinson doesn't take enough care of himself.

Yet, *How tawdry*, he thinks, when he thinks of ill-health.

Sinusitis, colitis, stress disorders: dirty suits he can't take off.

He's not afraid of pain, per se, but rather the anticipatory fear of pain.

It's not until he sees blood with the piss in the toilet water that he finally goes in.

The consulting room is stilted, airless.

The doctor says his condition is *involute*—just another way to say *it's complicated*.

He must stay for a week to be sure the meds work.

How perverse to be so sick when the weather's so clement.

Robinson's self-pity can only be gratuitous, but he knows it's gratuitous. So.

From his window he watches sun glint off the kidney-shaped pool in the courtyard.

The sleeping pill makes it so hard to stay awake.

Robinson really does remember a time when things were more wholesome.

But it's an invented memory he sees in his delirium: sweet corn swaying in a backyard breeze.

The good feelings of the past fall away in a striptease.

# ROBINSON SENDS A LETTER TO SOMEONE

*Cento XIII*

I have a fearful hangover from too many orange blossoms,
but will see if I can subdue this typewriter anyway.
                    I should know better.
I have been working like one possessed & have done
a couple of new canvases since you were here.
Hope this productivity keeps up; it makes all the difference
between the manic & the depressive, as Santayana
once remarked to Bud Freeman.
                    Yr. last letter came at a time
when I cd. really use it: Don't think I wrote you
that I was ill a while back & in the hospital for a brief stretch,
but quite okay now.
          The lacerating effects of middle age are dreadful,
God knows, but seem to me to differ only in kind
from those attending birth,
                         puberty,
                                  adolescence, etc.
For the last ten days or so I've been waking up
with maddening regularity at the crack of dawn,
wide awake & alert as Broyard at a showing
of pornographic movies.
                    My mind is batting on all eight
& there's nothing I can do but get up & work.
I suppose it's because I'm so damned snowed under
with things I feel ought to be done; but by midafternoon
I am slavering for a Spansule.
                    What the routes to wisdom
along this particular terrain are I wish I knew. The trick
of repeating, "It can't get any worse," is certainly no good,
when all the evidence points to quite the opposite.
Hope that things are going better than passably for you
in this attractive world of ours,

                   & in particular that those dexedrine
tablets I gave you made for a pleasanter, saner, & more euphoric
Thursday, after you left us here a long time back.

# ROBINSON'S DIVORCE

was a long time coming.
Yet, finalized, it stuns:

the manhole cover that flies
up & breaks your jaw.

Kids they never had, in-laws
he never saw, become a past

whose vastness he's only now
recognized. He never thought

of himself as the kind of man
who would have a first wife.

But there she is—his shade,
his failure. & there she'll be,

for the rest of his life.

# ROBINSON USES THIS SYMBOL TO SIGNIFY SEX

⊙

Bull's-eye or hex sign?
Vortex or breast?
A way to track frequency,
      he draws it obsessively
in the lattice of his calendar,
which has appeared to him lately
either as chain link fencing him in
or a ladder lowered to let him out of a trap.

⊙ here          ⊙ there          ⊙ wherever

But no matter with whom or how often,
      Robinson's brain retains its plots.
Adrift in the dark of his spotless apartment
atop black cotton sheets stained with cum
he knows ⊙ won't save him.
      Still he slaves for it.
⊙ lets him forget for a moment—
then remember—how it feels to be
fleshly.      Animal.      Dumb.

# ROBINSON SENDS A LETTER TO SOMEONE

*Cento XIV*

       Had any interesting dreams?
I am discouraged, indeed, about my own dream-life—
repetitive & moth-eaten—so tiresome
I'd give a good deal not to have them any more.
           Still they come:

       The party had a peculiar quality of horror
I shall not soon forget—John's place—magnificent,
       but something strange about it.
Knocked at the door—no answer, ajar. Yelled,
       but the house seemed deserted.
           Inside:
cocktail glasses turned over, with spiderwebs in them;
       beds unmade.
       Soiled clothing littered the floors.
In the kitchen the sink was full of
       rusty knives.
In the icebox, butter turning green.
Something dripping in the basement.
       Went down.
       Found it half flooded.
Discovered a faucet running & turned it off.
       Prowled around
rather prepared to come upon a corpse or two.
       No one, dead or alive, was about.
           Finally left.

       I believe you owe me a letter.
           Later.

## STANDING ON THE LANDING

outside his apartment in Berkeley,
carpet graying, thoughts straying,

swimming through the murky pool
of light in the hall, Robinson tries

to recall his favorite joke from when
he worked circulation in the Denver

Public Library so long ago. Late
summer, late night. Can't get it right.

How the hell did it go? Feels like
someone's stuck a fork in his heart—

not the dinner kind, though, the kind
in the road: head to the new

girlfriend's house, or stay home?
Bennies or dexies? Roam

the Marina district, or drink alone?
Golden Gate or Mexico? Robinson

doesn't know. Maybe he'll do it all.
Reaches into his pocket, pops a small

red pill, then—oh, clarity! oh, recall!—
furrows of worry in his brow go slack:

*Man walks into a library,*
*asks for a book on suicide.*

*Librarian says, "Fuck you—*
*you won't bring it back."*

## ROBINSON CHEWS BLACKJACK GUM

The licorice stains his tongue
black. This cracks him up. The blue
pack makes him think of the plant's
pinnate leaves & spiked blue
flowers, how they grow, disorderly,
around the Tijuana border.
        He chews it medicinally,
stick after stick, hoping to smoke less,
to stop grinding his teeth. His temples
twitch with each chomp. This looks
like a tic. He imagines swallowing:
seven years to digest, seven years
bad luck.
            In the vertical
pool of the bathroom mirror,
his face appears to surface, green.
He smiles at his reflection: gums gray.
It's All Saints' Day—*Día de los Muertos*.
Robinson thinks again of Mexico.
What it would be like to live
in a country with a longer memory,
eating sugar coffins, bones of dough,
*anima* pastries shaped like souls.

# MONEY GIVES YOU CONFIDENCE,

Robinson's pretty sure,
but can't confirm—

he's never had enough.
Tough to get the week-

end off, but he's done it.
Stuffed himself aboard

the evening milk route
plane down to L.A.

He'll see his parents
in Santa Barbara,

but he won't stay
with them. Sunset.

Sky alight. Butane.
His mother waiting.

Her name's Sarah.
He calls her Sadie.

Infantilizing as ever,
though she'd never

realize, with her basket-
ful of fresh-baked

cookies. These days,
he's awake 20 hours

at a stretch. Tomorrow
he'll let her take him

for a shot of penicillin
for his sore throat

& bronchitis. He'll light
up a Pall Mall as soon

as they step outside
& she'll be appalled.

He'll borrow his father's
car, ride to Hollywood.

Spend Saturday night
in the garage of friends,

avoiding the couch,
so they don't notice

his wakefulness. Do
a little business. Fly

back to San Francisco.
Robinson doesn't

believe in luck. Doesn't
know whether struggling

makes you more free
or more trapped.

Takes a Nembutal.
Falls into his own bed.

Fitful & twitching
like an eyelid.

Amid rain that stops,
then starts again.

# ROBINSON SENDS A LETTER TO SOMEONE

*Cento XV*

That both you & John took pride in my accomplishments
& that what I have been able to do in both writing & painting
was a source of satisfaction & pride to you—
                                                                        up until now,
I have never had any indication that you thought otherwise.

I gather from your letter that you feel I have been wasting my time.

I must say that these days I am frequently assailed
with feelings that even efforts to produce art
are both heartbreaking & absurd.
                            But what else is there?

Thinking very seriously of taking off for Mexico.

I certainly do not feel defensive about my life or my way of life;
although I have made many mistakes, I have always tried
to the best of my ability to work hard & creative & as well
                                                            as I was able.

I don't speak out of any conceit, but with a certain amount of pride.

& if you know of anyone else, of any age, who has made something
of a reputation for himself in both literature & art,
                            I would like to know who it is.

I remember how pleased both John & you were when I got in *Who's
Who.*

How do you think I got there? If you think it has been easy
or without a struggle, or if you think it has all not been accompanied
by the blackest kind of doubts & despair—or that many times
I have wanted (but never for long) to chuck it all,

                                        you simply do not
                    know.

117

& believe me, I would never have taken a cent from you
if I hadn't believed it was given freely & with faith in my abilities.
There is no question of my gratitude.

## ROBINSON UNDERSTANDS AS HE STANDS AT NORTH POINT & FILLMORE

that forty years before, he'd be
standing in the bay—landfill

& earthquake rubble. His girl-
friend left a note on his door

this morning: *You are the one
to straighten me out. Would you?*

Instant distaste. Instinctive legs
striding the other way.

He doesn't want to be anywhere,
so he can't be "there" for her.

Around Marina Green, looking
rich & rumpled, Robinson

strolls. In a crumpled shirt
from yesterday, he's stumped.

*To commit to being fashionable
is to admit oneself perishable,*

the houses say. His ability to focus
is fleeting as an expletive.

Robinson tries to converge
on concretes: swans & breadcrusts,

the idle gentility of the buildings'
decay. *Let them fade*, he wants to say.

*Let them fade forever*. Lunches
at a PayLess Drugstore. Buys a bottle

of Jack Daniels to blunt excess
stimuli & truncate desire:

a corpse cut to fit its coffin.
Up to the sea, but not in today.

He can't get the world right,
he can only walk around in it.

# ROBINSON'S FRIENDS HAVE COME OVER FOR HIS 41ˢᵗ BIRTHDAY

The violet hour, the city at dusk.

His somnambulant apartment on Filbert Street.

Maybe this year will be frustrating in new ways—so much crap has yet to be pulled.

They bypass the folderol of candles, cake for the small divertimento of Ballantine Ale.

They eat pretzels & play some of Robinson's songs.

Four decades he's longed to be too good to ignore.

He bores himself these days.

Fears his conversion to a men's magazine cliché:

*Hot Jazz,* he thinks. *Liquor,* he thinks. *Dames, dames, dames.*

His actuality has become burlesque—

affection toward a stripper he met doing theater:

bleached blonde in lowgloss lip paint.

She's here, folded into a butterfly chair, wearing sexual darkness & a real mink stole.

Mysterious as a blank façade, Robinson has a moodswing.

Excuses himself to sit on the porch—

all misgiving & miscarried ambition.

Paging through a driving guide to Mexico.

Thinking: *I'm doing it again, applauding myself in an echoplex.*

Thinking: *Lifestyle, Libido, & Intellect.*

# THIS IS HOW ROBINSON FALLS ASLEEP

Robinson lies back
on the patchwork bedspread
like a burlap sack,

& the fan spinning light
across the cracked white ceiling
becomes a lantern

carried by his father upstairs,
then a flashlight in the nervous
hand of his ex-wife, drunk,

&, though reeling himself,
Robinson still feels enough to stare
even harder until all he sees

is a lighthouse across ice floes,
then a searchlight across snow dunes,
& at last he's lost from the furnished room.

# ROBINSON DINES MOSTLY IN RESTAURANTS LATELY

since he hates cooking alone
& hardly eats anyway. Bone-

thin in a linen suit, he executes
a slow vanishing act. Out West,

in the hinterlands, no one
ever walks. But after work,

Robinson's a one-man parade,
ambulating the tunnel under

the Santa Fe tracks to a hole-
in-the-wall his friends call

the best in town. He stops
for some Mexican food.

It's crudely rendered: a cool
taco & a cooler tamale

the consistency of a candle.
Takes a bromide pill chaser

to erase his nerves. Notes
an ad in the *Chronicle*:

"How to vacation in a kingly
style on a piggy bank budget"

at the Hotel del Coronado
in San Diego. So close to

Tijuana. He wants to go—
not there, but further.

He could be an aging gringo,
playing piano at a cantina

where no one speaks English.
The piano would be a Chicago

bordello type, with a majestic
& mellow bass. The salsa

makes his face sweat. He
settles the bill. The sun sets

behind the Standard Oil Refinery.
Robinson can't unlearn what he

already knows. But he could
start over in the afterglow.

# ROBINSON'S CAT

isn't Lonesome anymore, for
    nobody's around
to call him that.
      Alone in the rooms'
Robinsonian aftermath
    the somnolent creature
misses his master, as much
    as his short cat memory
permits. Mirrors on the walls
    have become dark lakes;
they will never reflect
    Robinson's face again,
& words in the books
    have been replaced
with white space since Robinson's
    never returning to read them.
The cat scales the table,
    bats at anonymous bills
whose address blanks
    would fill were Robinson
to re-enter. Cat-face turned down
    in a cat-faced frown,
the cat walks the keys of the piano
    all night, longing
for a hand to gently remove him.
    His owner was silent
when he left, black eyes burning
    with desperate alacrity—
but what can a cat know
    of setbacks & letdowns?
All he's learned for sure is that
    nobody hears him,
& although sometimes trouble
    can be terribly loud,
other times it can surround you
    with no sound at all.

# HISTORICALLY, SUICIDES

are said to have been buried on the north sides of churches—with criminals, the convicted, & infants, unbaptized.

Robinson likes to park on the north side of the bridge.

To put his feet on the footpath, where the drop begins, terminus of an experiment's Westward expansion.

To look at America the hustler, the wheeler-dealer.

At a world gone rotten, & his own inutility.

The futility of futility.

To think *Goddamn it.*

Profanity's not just for people with a limited vocabulary.

A concordance of Robinson's recent conversations would reveal the words most used to be *silence* & *away.*

He's just made the final payment on the Plymouth & knows he should not be feeling this way.

Soaked in bathos. Like taking a bath.

The water below grim & inappropriate as dark gray wool in July.

Repeated thoughts, repeated gestures—

perfervid. Very fervid. Extremely ardent.

A quote that's been underlined, starred, then underlined again.

The city through the fog, near & shiny, but seeming so distant.

Pellucid. Very lucid. Extremely clear.

A silvery atmosphere of faded dreams & intangible regret.

The people he's befriended there, with condescension, neurotic & tea-smoking lightweights.

The ardor with which he will miss his real friends.

Who know he is a self-confessed to-do list addict.

Who will see this date, later, circled in his calendar.

Hope, Robinson reasons, is a cruel disease & he's finally over it.

He will go out glitzed. Called a phenom. Called unstoppable.

Will the last to leave the city please turn out the lights?

# ROBINSON'S TELEPHONE RINGS

the Tuesday after he last was seen.

A policeman is there to pick the shrill thing up.

*Who is it?* the couple of friends present ask as he cups it to his ear.

Then hangs up. There was no one there.

They have come to recon a vacant property—a *mise en scène:*

Knoll butterfly chairs—a pair of them—

two red socks soaking in the white bathroom sink,

a saucer of milk for the cat to drink,

a stack of reel-to-reel tapes,

a matchbook from the Italian Village where he ate his last spaghetti dinner,

& two books he'd been re-reading, or wanted someone to think he had:

*The Devils* & *The Tragic Sense of Life.*

Preoccupation & a certain mode of self-presentation.

Even when absent, Robinson has a style.

No wallet, though. No watch, no sleeping bag, no bankbook.

The apartment looks the way it feels to read a newspaper that's one day old.

The policeman wants to go back outside, among the lemons & fog & barking dogs.

Out where the sun can copper their faces.

Writing takes space, recordings take time.

The place puts the policeman in mind of something he read recently, about the collapse of a dead star.

About how it takes ages for the light to become motionless.

Seven years after a disappearance, a person can be pronounced dead.

But that's nothing compared to the size of the ocean.

Kathleen Rooney is a founding editor of Rose Metal Press, and the author of six books of poetry and nonfiction, including most recently the essay collection *For You, For You I Am Trilling These Songs* (Counterpoint, 2010) and the memoir *Live Nude Girl: My Life as an Object* (University of Arkansas Press, 2009). She lives in Chicago.

# Afterword

Sometimes an optimist is one of the saddest things a person can be. Weldon Kees (1914-1955?), poet and disappearee, may be one of the saddest optimists ever.

In his introduction to Kees' *Collected Poems*, Donald Justice writes that Kees is "one of the bitterest poets in history," and that "the bitterness may be traced to a profound hatred for a botched civilization, Whitman's America come to a dead end on the shores of the Pacific."

The title of this book comes from a line—"Robinson alone provides the image Robinsonian"—in Kees' poem "Robinson," which originally appeared in the *New Yorker* in 1945; the poem depicts the title character's unsettling absence.

Robinson is—not unlike Berryman's "Henry" of 14 years later—a kind of quasi-alter ego. Robinson, appearing in a mere four poems, is a cosmopolitan man

> in Glen plaid jacket, Scotch-grain shoes,
> Black four-in-hand and oxford button-down,
> The jeweled and silent watch that winds itself, the brief-
> Case, covert topcoat, clothes for spring, all covering
> His sad and usual heart, dry as a winter leaf.

In "Return of the Ghost," Kees writes:

> Your absence breeds
> A longer silence through the rooms. We haunt ourselves.

Justice writes of Kees, "If the whole of poetry can be read as a denial of the values of the present civilization, as I believe it can, then the disappearance of Kees becomes as symbolic an act as Rimbaud's flight or Crane's suicide." His life and work add up to more than any single decision.

Kathleen Rooney
Chicago, IL

CPSIA information can be obtained at www.ICGtesting.com
Printed in the USA
BVOW041446181112

305815BV00001B/20/P